3 4028 08964 7771
HARRIS COUNTY PUBLIC LIBRARY

W9-CHI-607

BY GAIL GIBBONS

THE MOON BOOK

New and Updated

HOLIDAY HOUSE · NEW YORK

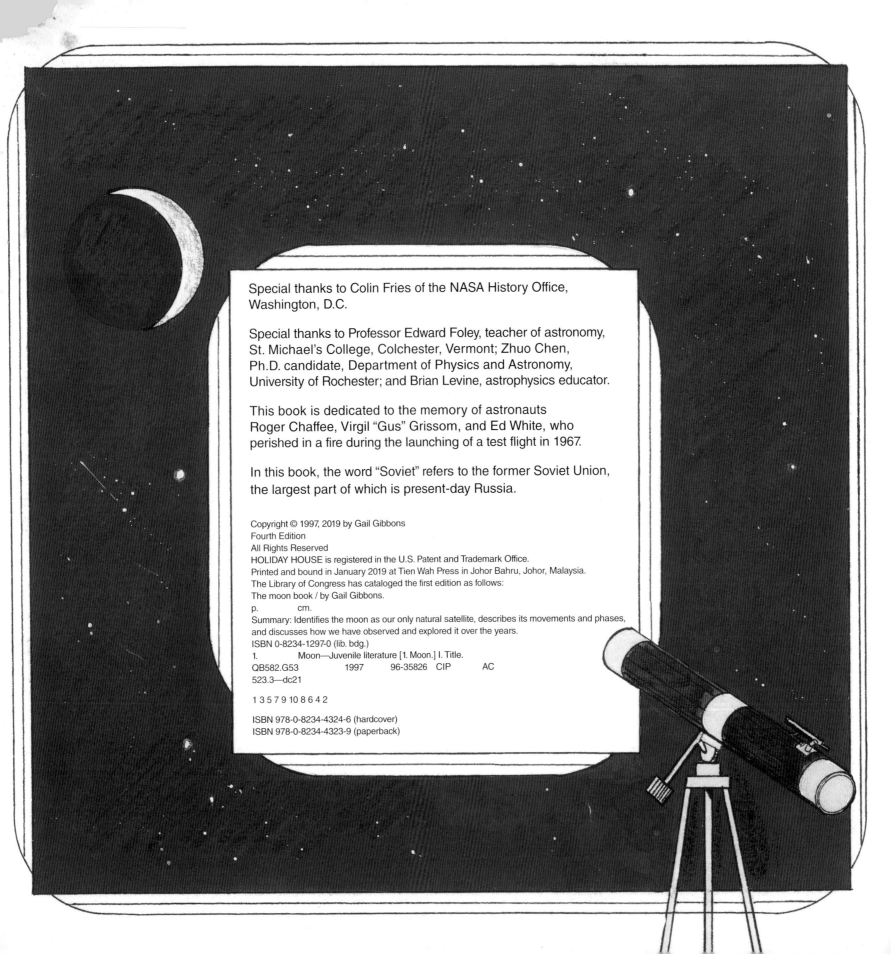

Special thanks to Colin Fries of the NASA History Office,
Washington, D.C.

Special thanks to Professor Edward Foley, teacher of astronomy,
St. Michael's College, Colchester, Vermont; Zhuo Chen,
Ph.D. candidate, Department of Physics and Astronomy,
University of Rochester; and Brian Levine, astrophysics educator.

This book is dedicated to the memory of astronauts
Roger Chaffee, Virgil "Gus" Grissom, and Ed White, who
perished in a fire during the launching of a test flight in 1967.

In this book, the word "Soviet" refers to the former Soviet Union,
the largest part of which is present-day Russia.

MOON

As the sun sets at the end of each day, the sky becomes darker and darker. On many clear nights our moon shines brightly in the night sky.

A STAR burns gases that give off heat and light. The SUN is a star.

The MOON reflects sunlight, it does not shine like a star. The moon revolves around Earth.

Our moon is the brightest and biggest light in our night sky. It outshines all the stars and planets, which appear as small points of light. Some planets have many moons. Earth has one.

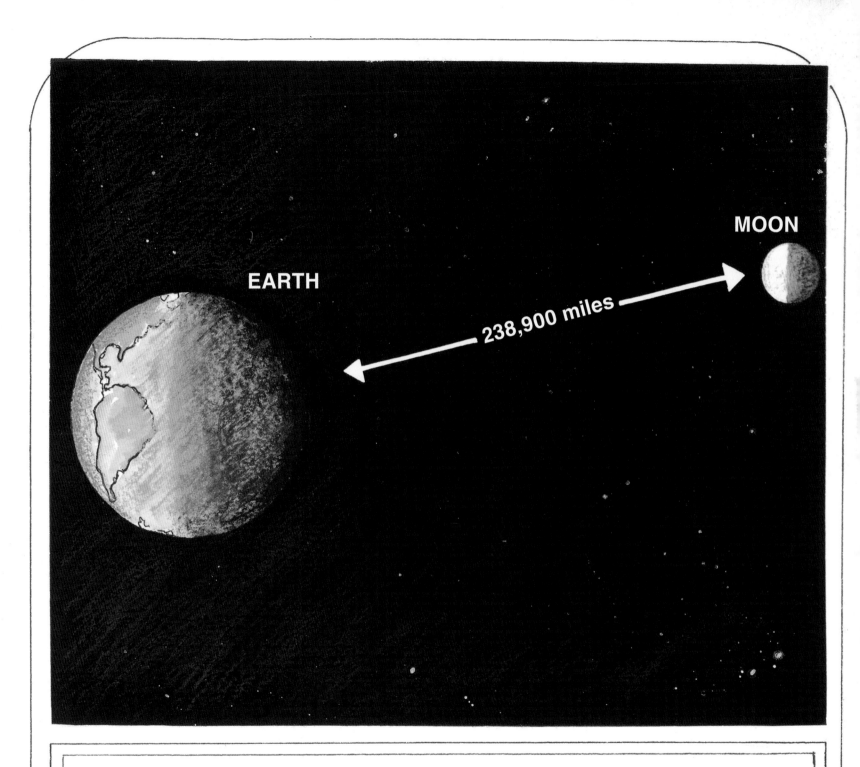

Our moon looks big and bright because it is so close to Earth compared to the faraway stars and planets. It is about 238,900 miles (384,000 km) away.

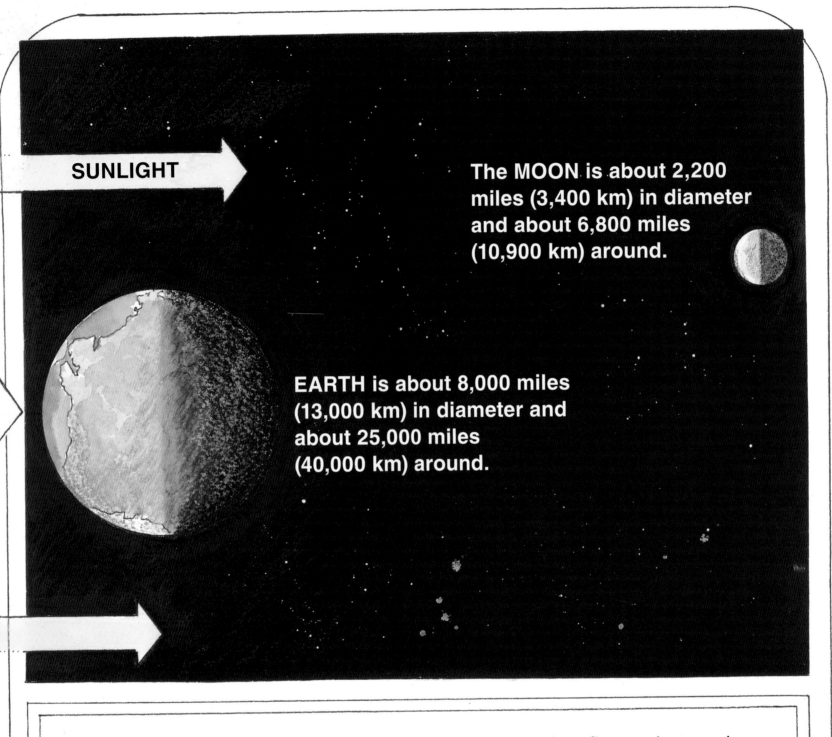

SUNLIGHT

The MOON is about 2,200 miles (3,400 km) in diameter and about 6,800 miles (10,900 km) around.

EARTH is about 8,000 miles (13,000 km) in diameter and about 25,000 miles (40,000 km) around.

The moon is bright in the night sky because it reflects the sun's light. It is about one-fourth the size of Earth. It is made up of rock and dust. There is no air, no liquid water, or sign of life.

ASTRONOMERS are scientists who study things in space like planets, moons, and stars.

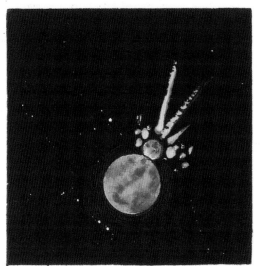

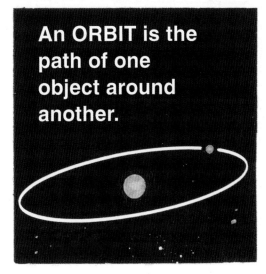

An ORBIT is the path of one object around another.

Astronomers have discovered that the moon is 4.51 billion years old, just slightly younger than Earth. Something probably collided with Earth and tossed out a cloud of rock and debris. While orbiting around Earth, the rock and debris came together to form the moon.

In ancient times, people thought the moon was a powerful god or goddess. The Romans called their moon goddess Diana. In Greece, the moon goddess was Artemis, who rode through the sky in a silver chariot.

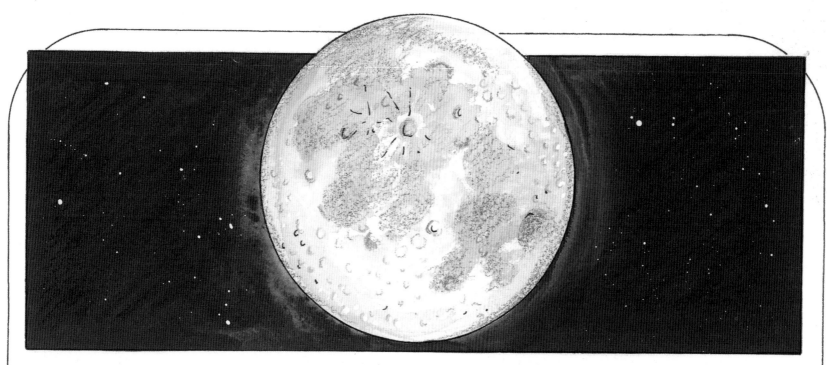

Stories and legends were told about the shapes and shadows that show on the moon's surface. Some people said the moon showed a man's face, the "man in the moon" who was imprisoned there for stealing. Others told of moon demons living there.

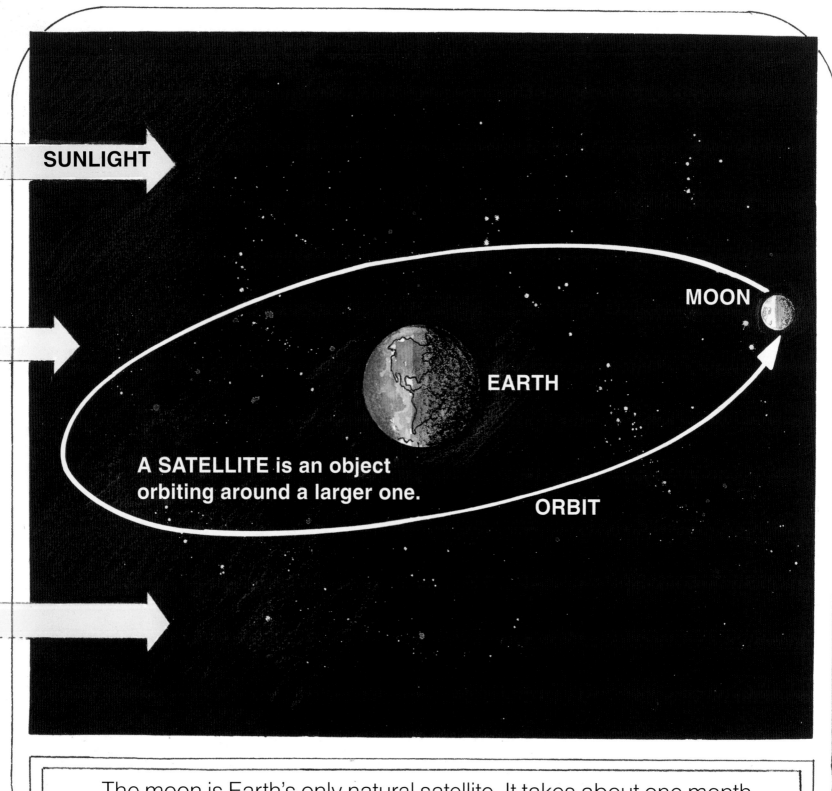

SUNLIGHT

MOON

EARTH

A SATELLITE is an object orbiting around a larger one.

ORBIT

The moon is Earth's only natural satellite. It takes about one month for the moon to travel around Earth.

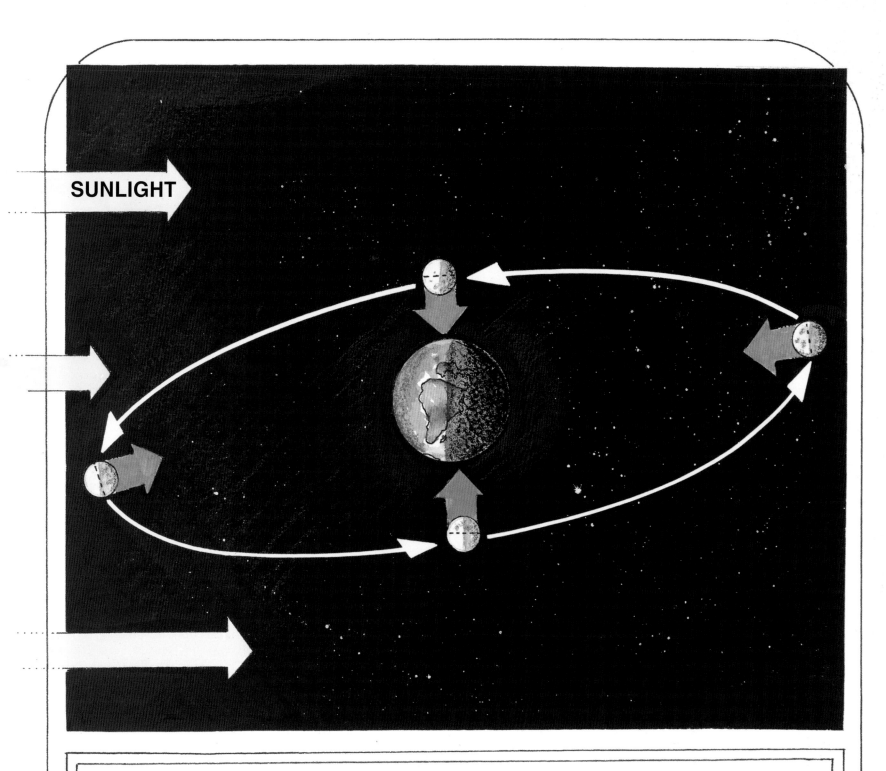

SUNLIGHT

The moon also spins only once as it orbits Earth. This causes the same side to always face our planet. One "day" on the moon lasts about 28 Earth days because the moon spins so slowly.

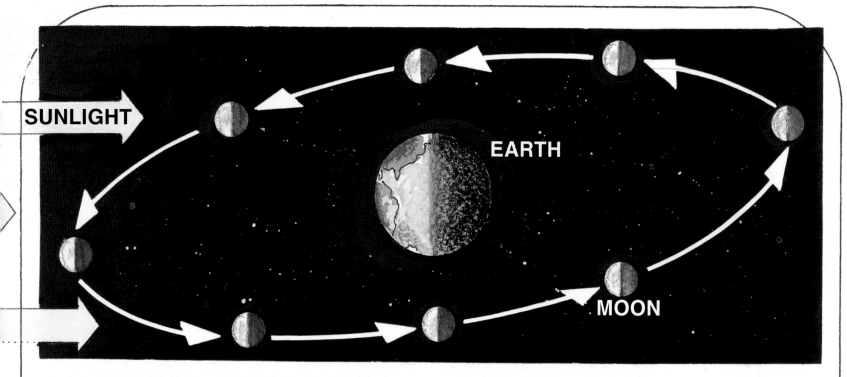

The moon appears to change shape, but it doesn't. The different shapes we see are called phases of the moon. We are seeing different amounts of light being reflected on the moon. How much light we see depends on the positions of Earth, moon, and sun.

PHASES OF THE MOON

NEW MOON

During a new moon, the moon is almost directly between the sun and Earth. The moon looks dark. We see no reflected light.

CRESCENT MOON

The moon is WAXING when the lit surface we see is getting bigger.

In a few days, a bit of the sunlit side of the moon shows. It forms a crescent.

FIRST-QUARTER MOON

When the moon is a quarter of its way around Earth, it is in its first-quarter phase. We see it as half-lit. It is sometimes called a half moon.

GIBBOUS MOON

When the moon is waxing between a first-quarter moon and a full moon, it is called a gibbous moon.

FULL MOON

About two weeks have passed since the new moon. Now the entire face of the moon we see shines.

GIBBOUS MOON

The moon is WANING when the lit surface we see is getting smaller.

When the moon is waning between a full moon and a last-quarter moon, it is a gibbous moon once again.

LAST-QUARTER MOON

When the moon is three-quarters of its way around Earth, it is in its last-quarter phase. Again we see it as half-lit. It is sometimes called a half moon.

CRESCENT MOON

Once again we see a small sliver of moon shining in the sky.

NEW MOON

It takes the moon about one month to go through its entire set of phases. People used to know the time of the month by watching the moon's phases.

SOLAR ECLIPSE

SUNLIGHT

As the moon orbits Earth, it passes between the sun and Earth as a new moon. Sometimes, the moon lines up just right and casts a shadow on Earth. This is called a solar eclipse.

A SOLAR ECLIPSE PROJECT

Here's how to make a sun "projector" to see a picture of a solar eclipse.

WARNING! Never look directly at a solar eclipse. The sun's rays can hurt your eyes.

1. Poke a pin through the center of a piece of heavy paper that is a little bigger than this book. This is your projector.

2. Stand with your back to the sun. Hold the "projector" at your shoulder so sunlight shines through the hole.

3. Hold another piece of heavy paper in your other hand. This is your screen.

4. Move both papers until an image of the eclipse appears on the screen.

The moon's shadow falls on Earth. A solar eclipse can last up to seven and one-half minutes.

LUNAR ECLIPSE

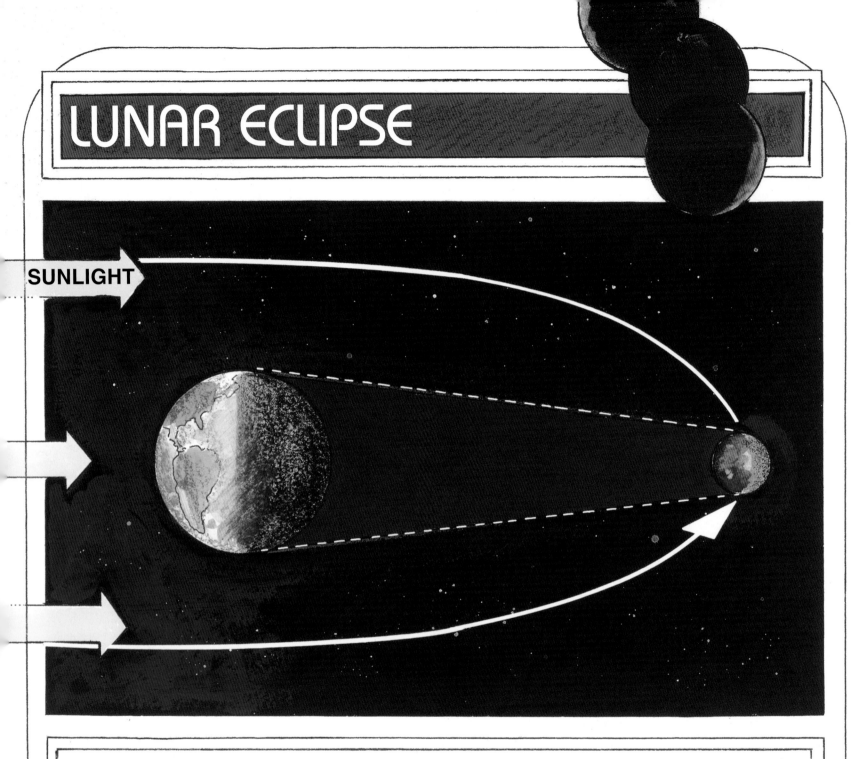

SUNLIGHT

When the sun, Earth, and moon are exactly lined up, a lunar eclipse happens. As in a solar eclipse, the moon's orbit is not tilted. Earth blocks off the sunlight that usually lights up the moon. The moon has a reddish glow.

"Lunar" comes from "Luna," the Latin word for moon. All stages of the lunar eclipse can take up to about six hours.

A HIGH TIDE happens about every 13 hours.

The moon affects the oceans, too. The moon's pull, called gravity, on the oceans is strong enough to cause tides. Tides are the daily rising and falling of the oceans' waters.

This is because the moon takes about 25 hours to come back to the same place in the sky it was the night before. Tide differences vary around the world.

BINOCULARS

TELESCOPE

OBSERVATORY

Some night-sky gazers and astronomers can get a close-up view of the moon by looking through binoculars. Others look through telescopes. Some huge telescopes are used at observatories.

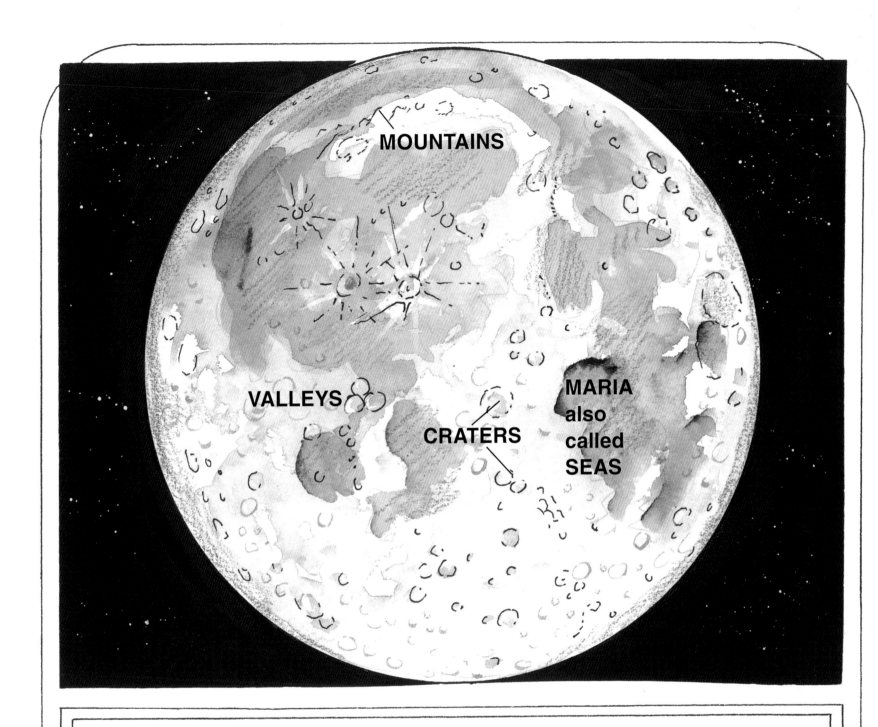

A close-up view of the moon's surface shows dark patches astronomers call maria. Other areas are covered with craters, mountains, and valleys. The oldest identified moon crater is about 2 billion years old.

LUNA 3

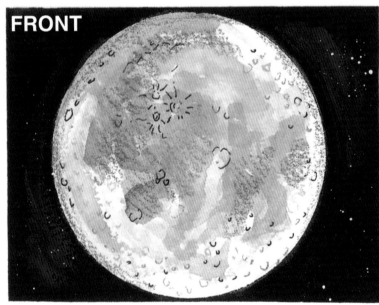

FRONT

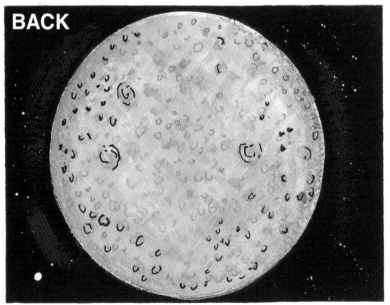

BACK

For centuries people have wanted to know more about our moon. In 1959, the Soviet spacecraft Luna 3 transmitted to Earth the first pictures of the far side, or back, of the moon. There aren't as many dark areas on that side as on the side we see from Earth.

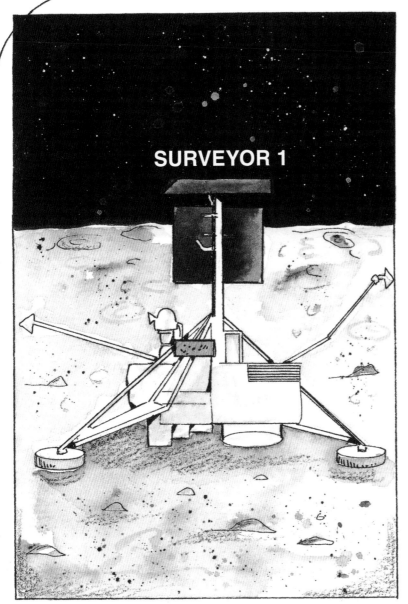

SURVEYOR 1

APOLLO 8

In 1961 President John F. Kennedy made a commitment to put Americans on the moon before the end of the decade. At first many American unmanned spacecraft were sent. Pictures were taken. Then Surveyor 1 landed on the moon in 1966. It sent back information about the moon's surface. The first manned orbit of the moon was made by Apollo 8 astronauts in 1968.

On July 20, 1969, Neil Armstrong and Edwin "Buzz" Aldrin of the Apollo 11 mission became the first men to walk on the moon.

There were five more Apollo landings on the moon. The last one, Apollo 17, was in 1972. The astronauts did experiments and gathered samples. Astronomers and other scientists were able to learn more about the history and nature of our moon.

On a clear night when the moon is in the sky, gaze up at it. We are still learning more about our closest neighbor . . .

the moon.

MOON MILESTONES

About 4200 years ago People in ancient Mesopotamia thought that a lunar eclipse was a bad omen, meaning the king was going to die.

About 2500 years ago A Greek philosopher, Anaxagoras, was the first to theorize that the moon's light came from the sun, and he was imprisoned for it.

About 2200 years ago A Greek astronomer, Aristarchus, figured a way to measure the distance from Earth to the moon.

About 2000 years ago A Syrian philosopher, Posidonius, explained the effect the moon has on tides.

1609 The Italian scientist, Galileo, used a telescope to study the moon. He was the first to write that the moon has mountains and valleys.

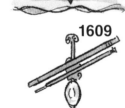

1647 Hevelius, a pioneer of moon mapping, charted more than 250 formations on the moon.

1850s The first telescope-based pictures of the moon may have been taken by William Bond and J. Whipple in the United States.

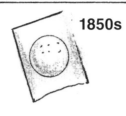

1920s A French astronomer, Bernard Lyot, concluded that the moon's surface was made of dust.

1959 The Soviet spacecraft Luna 2 was the first spacecraft to reach the moon. It crash landed. Luna 3 took pictures of the far side of the moon.

1966 The Soviet's Luna 9 was the first spacecraft to make a soft landing on the moon. It was also the first object to transmit a signal to Earth from another celestial object.

1968 The first manned orbit of the moon was made by Apollo 8.

July 20, 1969 Neil Armstrong, the first man to set foot on the moon, said, "That's one small step for man, one giant leap for mankind."

MOON LEGENDS AND STORIES

Egyptians said the moon was the god Osiris, who died and came back to life each month.

The Cherokee Nation held the Great New Moon Festival around October to mark the beginning of the Cherokee New Year.

The ancient Chinese believed the goddess Chang'E lived forever on the moon. The Chinese eat mooncakes in her honor each year at the mid-Autumn moon festival.

Some people used to think the moon was made of cheese because of the shapes and shadows on the moon's surface.

The ancient Vikings believed the dark shapes on the moon were of a girl and boy who were kidnapped while getting a bucket of water.

"Hey Diddle Diddle," the nursery rhyme, has a famous line, "the cow jumped over the moon."

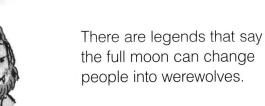

There are legends that say the full moon can change people into werewolves.

MORE MOON FACTS

In Britain, France, and Ireland, ancient stone circles have been found that line the viewer up with the rising and setting positions of the moon.

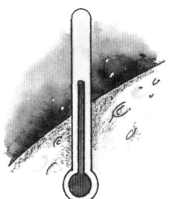

The temperature on the moon varies greatly. Scientists estimate that it may rise as high as 200 degrees Fahrenheit (about 100 degrees Celsius) and fall as low as -250 degrees F (about -120 degrees C).

Gravity on the moon's surface is about one-sixth of Earth's gravity. That means if you can leap five feet on Earth, you could leap thirty feet if you were on the moon.

The largest crater visible to us on Earth is the Bailly crater. It is 183 miles (295 km) across.

842 pounds (382 kg) of moon rocks were brought back by Apollo astronauts.

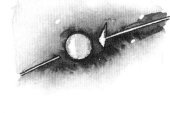

The moon travels in its orbit at about 2,300 miles (3,700 km) per hour.

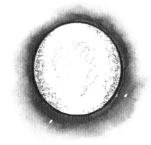

When there are two full moons within the same month, the second full moon is called a blue moon. This happens about every two to two and one-half years.

The "harvest" moon is the moon closest to the first day of fall, on September 22nd or 23rd.

On many clear days, we can see the moon in our daylight sky.